Maïte Roche

The Gospel
for little children

CTS Children's Books

Maïte Roche

The Gospel
for little children

God chose
Mary.
She said 'Yes'
to the angel.
She would be
the mother of
Jesus, the
long awaited
Saviour,
the promised
Son of God.

In Bethlehem,
Jesus was
born. He was
laid in
a manger.
The shepherds
came to
adore him.
He came for
all men.
Joy and
Peace to all!
It's Christmas!

Jesus grew in
strength and
wisdom in his
family
with Joseph
and Mary.
God's love
was with him.

When Jesus was twelve years old, he spoke about God, his Father, to the priests and learned men in the Temple of Jerusalem.

When Jesus was thirty, he was baptised by John the Baptist in the waters of the Jordan. The Holy Spirit descended on him like a dove and God said, "This is my beloved Son."

Jesus called the twelve apostles. He said to them, "Come". Peter, Andrew, James and John followed him, then Philip, Thomas, Matthew, Bartholomew, James, Jude, Simon – and also Judas.

Little children
and grown ups,
poor people
and beggars,
came from
everywhere to
listen to Jesus.
He taught them:
"Love God your
Father and love
each other,
because you are
all brothers."

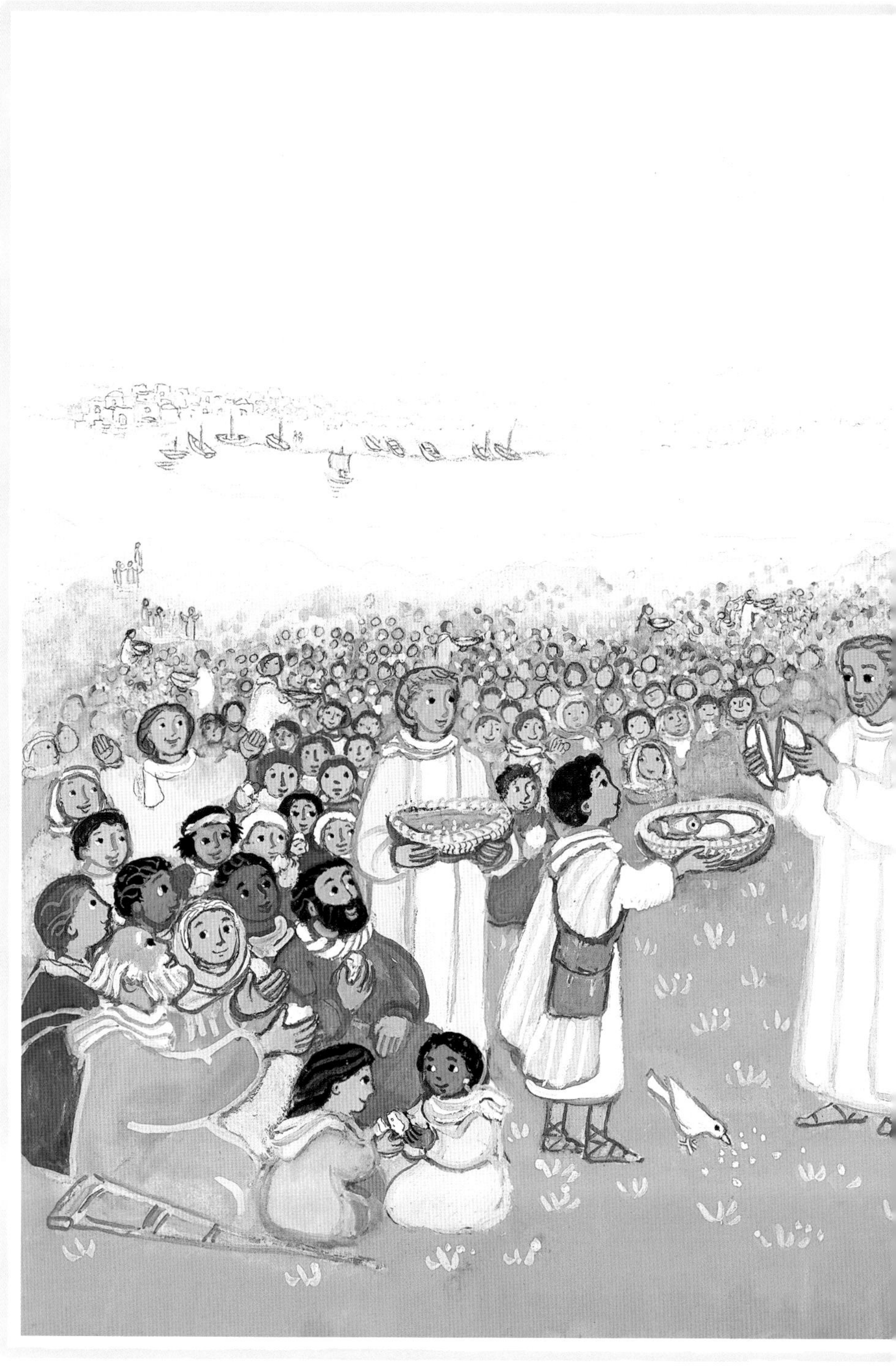

It was evening. The people were hungry. There were only five loaves and two fish to eat, brought by a little boy. Jesus took them and blessed them. He shared them out and five thousand people were fed!

A storm raged. The boat was in danger. "Help! Jesus, save us!" cried the disciples. Jesus replied: "Don't be afraid my friends. I am with you." Jesus commanded the storm to stop and all was calm.

To little
children
Jesus says,
"Come to me.
God loves
you and
blesses you."
God forgives
and heals you,
and to those
who believe in
him, he gives
eternal life.

Here is Jesus, coming on a little grey donkey. The road to Jerusalem was covered with cloaks and palms. "Hosannah!" sang his friends. "Hosannah! Blessed is he who comes in the name of the Lord."

The table was prepared for the festival meal. Jesus blessed the bread and shared it out. "Take and eat. This is my body, given for you." Jesus blessed the wine and gave it to them. "Take this and drink it. This is my blood poured out for you."

Betrayed by
Judas, Jesus
was handed
over to
the soldiers.
He had to carry
the heavy
cross.
Mary, John and
some friends
were near him.
Jesus died
on the cross.
He gave his
life for love
of us all.

alleluia!

Three days later on Easter morning, the women came to the tomb. They were carrying perfumes and spices. An angel said to them, "Jesus isn't here any more. He has risen from the dead! Go and tell the others." They left full of joy. "Jesus is alive. Alleluia!"

Before going to the Father, Jesus blessed his apostles and said to them, "You will receive strength from the Holy Spirit, and you will go throughout the world announcing the love of God to all my brothers. And I will be with you every day, to the end of time."

CTS Children's Books

The Beautiful Story of Jesus, *by Maïte Roche*
(ISBN 978 1 86082 492 0 CTS Code CH 13)

The Beautiful Story of Mary, *by Maïte Roche*
(ISBN 978 1 86082 762 4 CTS Code CH 37)

The Beautiful Story of the Bible, *by Maïte Roche*
(ISBN 978 1 86082 675 7 CTS Code CH 27)

Benedict & Chico, *by Jeanne Perego*
(ISBN 978 1 86082 493 7 CTS Code CH 12)

The Bible for little children, *by Maïte Roche*
(ISBN 978 1 86082 399 2 CTS Code CH 2)

Faith for children, *by Christine Pedotti*
(ISBN 978 1 86082 447 0 CTS Code CH 9)

First prayers for little children, *by Maïte Roche*
(ISBN 978 1 86082 447 0 CTS Code CH 9)

Getting to Know God, *by Christine Pedotti*
(ISBN 978 1 86082 762 4 CTS Code CH 37)

The Most Beautiful Christmas Story, *by Maïte Roche*
(ISBN 978 1 86082 446 3 CTS Code CH 8)

My Simple Mass Book, *by CTS*
(ISBN 978 1 86082 878 2 CTS Code CH 48)

Prayers around the Crib, *by Juliette Levivier*
(ISBN 978 1 86082 445 6 CTS Code CH 7)

Praying at Mass, *by Juliette Levivier*
(ISBN 978 1 86082 491 3 CTS Code CH 11)

Praying with Mary, *by Juliette Levivier*
(ISBN 978 1 86082 536 1 CTS Code CH 14)

Praying with the Holy Spirit, *by Juliette Levivier*
(ISBN 978 1 86082 537 8 CTS Code CH 15)

Praying with the first Chritians, *by Juliette Levivier*
(ISBN 978 1 86082 490 6 CTS Code CH 10)

Praying with the friends of Jesus, *by Juliette Levivier*
(ISBN 978 1 86082 444 9 CTS Code CH 6)

The Rosary, *by Juliette Levivier*
(ISBN 978 1 86082 397 8 CTS Code CH 3)

The Way of the Cross, *by Juliette Levivier*
(ISBN 1 86082 398 X CTS Code CH 4)

The Gospel for little children: Published 2006 by the Incorporated Catholic Truth Society, 40-46 Harleyford Road, London SE11 5AY. Tel: 020 7640 0042; Fax: 020 7640 0046; www.CTSbooks.org Copyright © 2006 the Incorporated Catholic Truth Society in this English language edition.

ISBN: 978 1 86082 400 5   CTS Code CH 1

L'Evangile pour les petits: by Maïte Roche, published 2002 by Groupe Fleurus-Mame, 15-27 rue Moussorgski, 75018 Paris; ISBN 2-7289-1002-2. Copyright © Groupe Fleurus 2002.